ROYAL MENU: on a budget

VEGAN: Playful & Uplifting Foods!

By: Eddy Coleson

This book is rather a consolidation of my own journey towards a more natural, simple lifestyle that is designed to inspire, and ignite culinary creativity in anyone willing to meet their potential halfway. This gift lies dormant within all of us longing to come out and play, while simultaneously building a strong foundation towards a great life, a better future for ourselves, as well as that of the next generations.
Of course let's not forget the future of our only home, Mother Nature.

Other than that, welcome to my world.

Photography - designs / ideas: Eddy Coleson

Dedication

A truly special THANK YOU from my heart to my friends and family for believing in me on this journey together. I cherish your existence, care, appreciation, and encouragement.

From me to YOU - may what's in this book bring inspiration, joy & happiness, not merely in the kitchen but also in other areas of life just as much as it has done and will continue to do in my own life.

I hope you also see it as a fun journey while looking through the pages, rather than just another book with recipes in it.
Thus allow it to stimulate the child & playfulness in you.

– Stay well!

We've all heard about the benefits of fasting, but how many really go on and do it without feelings of guilt- right..? It seems as if the thought alone causes anxiety, which promotes even more confusion (you can probably relate to the dramatic image on the following page).

So I've decided to put together a book to inform & inspire people who struggle with (intermittent) fasting, or those who like it awesome, creative and simple but just don't know what to eat that can keep them satisfied, healthy, and not stuffed or exhausted during the day. A lot of people would love to eat healthy, home-cooked, vegetarian or vegan, and natural every day but there are so many different aspects that stand in the way regardless of one's class or age. So why not focus on one meal that is rich and tasty rather than eating multiple meals throughout the day that are halfhearted or boring, which are also likely to cause constipation, inflammations, and regret along the way – right..?

Eating shouldn't merely be a survival issue, thus this book is about focusing on just one really good meal that awakens a sense of empowerment- aiming at organic, gluten, sugar & guilt-free. Consolidating 3 traditional meals into 1 will save you money, energy in the body, and allow cells to regenerate properly while having fun at the same time.
<< The truth of the matter is that most people eat once a day anyway, the rest of the time it is usually little things they're not proud of and it's because of lack of energy (stolen by the heavy meals) hoping that coffee/snacks/sodas, etc. will boost them, only to end up in a deep and perpetual cycle of seeking the sweetest & cheapest solution possible; which almost always turns out to be the most expensive slip-ups later in life. >>

You'll also find some powerful, healing delicious juice/smoothie recipes, and desserts as well in this book for the sweet tooth, of course. :-)

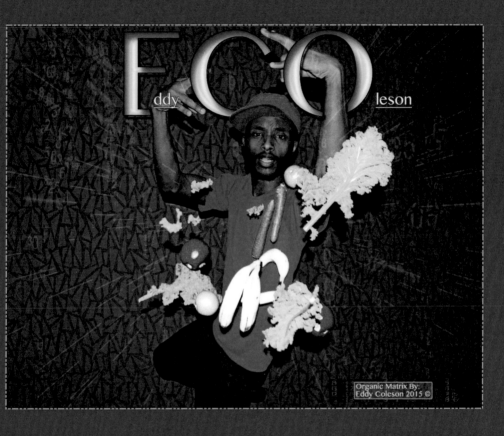

ECO

Eddy   Coleson

Organic Matrix By:
Eddy Coleson 2015 ©

We all want to make & enjoy fun healthy meals, but the struggle is very real!
There's that time issue syndrome, and then there are the norms, obstacles of all
kinds, distractions, lack of information & inspiration, – you name it.. And no one is
exempt in this system we've built around us! — We're in this together.

Table Of Contents

Fresh & Sunny

What you need:
- A juicer / Slow-Juicer.
- If you make it in a blender, you'll need a cheesecloth or something similar with extremely tiny holes to separate the pulp and the juice while squeezing.

Fun facts:
Did you know orange juice is not only a powerful source of Vitamin C, but it also contains *Folate* (vitamin B-9), which is important in red blood cell formation and for healthy cell growth and function.
Let's not forget *Potassium* which regulates fluid balance, muscle contractions, and nerve signals. It reduces blood pressure and water retention, protects against stroke, and prevents osteoporosis and kidney stones. - Doesn't this just make you feel like getting a few glasses already?

Ingredients
½ a Lemon
3 medium Oranges
1 inch of fresh Ginger
1 inch of fresh Turmeric

Directions
Peel the oranges, leaving as much of the white part inside between the skin and fruit, (as it contains even more vitamin C & other important nutrients).
Now start the juicer and begin to gradually inserting pieces of the oranges in it.
Add ginger, turmeric, and lemon.
— When done juicing, pour into a glass and enjoy chilled or right away.

If you'd like an even more powerful drink, add a handful of Cilantro, which is one of the greatest detoxifying agents for the removal of toxins, and heavy metals from the body. - Tastes heavenly too!

Watermelon Paradise

It can either be made in a blender, and then strained through a cheesecloth / strainer to separate the juice from the pulp, or in a slow-juicer.

Watermelon, a fruit that truly loves your heart.

– <u>Facts about Heart health</u>:
According to statistics there are more people who die from heart related issues on Mondays than on any other day of the week.
– (Do what loves YOU)!

Ingredients
4 cups of Watermelon, or
(½ a medium Melon).
A handful of fresh Mint.
½ a medium Lime/Lemon.

Directions
<u>In a juicer</u>: add the pieces of watermelon and start juicing. Throw in some mint leaves, add the lime with or without skin. Pour into a glass, add a few freshly picked mint leaves to it, and enjoy a really fresh, very simple and unforgettable taste.

If you make it in a blender, you'll need to strain it thoroughly.

Watermelon thanks to its over 90% pure water content, makes it the most hydrating fruit. It is packed with amino acids & an organic compound called lycopene which is great for heart health. — Isn't the color just magnificent?

Your *heart* spells: [E.A.R.T.H] for a reason. Give it life.

The Life Force

It has become more and more difficult to drink water for many of us. Therefore I found a way to make it easier & enjoyable for the body to absorb, while enjoying in the process. Adding fruits and berries to the water gives you a vitamin boost. It is the way to go when making your own vitamin-infused water.

It is the best solution in terms of hydration, it comes on the second place after fresh juice which is the purest form of water (called: H3O2, fourth phase of water with the same molecular structure as spring water). Also known as: "Structured Water".

- Facts: As humans, we were designed to drink spring water from nature in its natural purest form, unfortunately, we've adapted to drinking water that is recycled and comes through pipes filled with chemicals & other contaminants that deprive it of essential minerals.

Ingredients
Water
Fruits/Citrus/Berries
(Thyme, Basil), etc.

Directions
Slice the fruits, etc.
Fill up a container with water, and add the slices into it.
Let sit for infusion, then enjoy a while later (or overnight for best results): chilled, with ice, or directly.

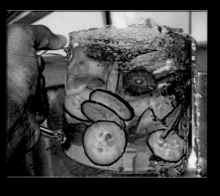

- Most water is H2O but groundbreaking research from Harvard and Cornell has found that **water in our cells and in plant cells is actually H3O2** – it is gel-like water charged by electrolytes. When touching most surfaces in the body, water transforms itself into so called Exclusion Zone (EZ) water, whose formula is H3O2.

There's a strong emphasis on imagery & presentation, simply because as humans we happen to be visual creatures. This means that our eyes make most of our decisions during the day, even though it may sound far-fetched.

That is how powerful images can be. We tend to want things that we see, and if we continue to be exposed, eventually whatever that is we're exposed to, ends up becoming part of our lives unconsciously.

F.Y.I:

It is scientifically proven that WATER has memory, and can record the vibrational state of the environment that it is found in or of the person handling it. This reminds us of why religion believed in blessing food before eating it. Since everything is frequency & vibration (energy), it makes sense that words or thoughts or even emotions have the power to affect the environment.
Now ask yourself "how much water is the human body made of?" Exactly, roughly 70% - 80%.
– We're literally walking talking tanks of water. Do yourself a favor and research: "Dr. Masaru Emoto", a scientist & expert in water memory, etc.

Not only does this delicious beverage cleanse the colon, but it is packed with vitamins and antioxidants, which help the body do its job without having to overwork whilst replenishing and rehydrating the cells. – Cheers!

EARTH is for HEART

Ingredients
½ a Lemon
1 Tangerine (or Orange)
2 Red Apples
(½ a Cucumber)
4 Celery Stalks
2 Inches of fresh Ginger

- For those who only have a blender (mixer) available, there's a possibility of squeezing the juice using a piece of cloth or a strainer with tiny holes after blending.

- Fun facts about Celery: It is an anti-inflammatory packed with fiber great for digestion, it helps lower cholesterol levels, and contains *flavonoids* (powerful antioxidant agents) that inhibit the growth of certain harmful bacteria.

Directions

Put all the ingredients into a juicer one after the other. Preferably a slow-juicer as it maintains the quality of the nutrients and squeezes most of the liquid out of the fruit more efficiently.

- (A centrifugal juicer works as well, though it doesn't extract 100% of the liquid from the fruits/veggies).

— You may enjoy this heavenly fresh drink either well chilled or directly.

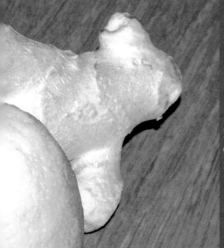

Psst.. Never be afraid to experiment with different ingredients! :-)

Solar-Plex-Juice

You need a Juicer / Slow-Juicer.

- <u>Grapefruit Facts</u>: It improves heart health, just like any citrus fruit it is packed with vitamin C. It reduces blood pressure and burns excessive / unwanted fat, making it a powerful detoxifier especially on an empty stomach. Mixing it with other equally powerful fruits & veggies makes it even more potent, leaving the cells properly hydrated and the body replenished.

Ingredients

1 inch of fresh Ginger
⅓ of a Grapefruit
½ a Cucumber
1 - 2 oranges

Directions

Put the ingredients in a juicer, one at a time.
Once ready, pour into a jug or any available container.
Serve directly in a drinking glass, with some ice, or preferably refrigerate beforehand.

- Peel the ingredients and slice them however it suits you or according to the size of your machine.

- Always begin with the softest ingredients when juicing.

This juice helped me overcome muscle cramps, constipation, back pains & most importantly; it improved my respiratory system.

- Facts: Beet greens are rich in nitrates, which have been shown to benefit lung function. Nitrates help relax blood vessels, reduce blood pressure, and optimize oxygen uptake. Since I no longer need eyewear, I'm almost certain that 80% of my eye health is thanks to the rich content of phytonutrients & especially the antioxidant lutein in beets, (see page: 106 - 107).

Ingredients
3 - 4 medium Beets
2 Oranges
½ a Lemon (or 1 Lime)
2 red Apples
2 inches of fresh Ginger
1 inch of Turmeric
A pinch of Black or,
Cayenne Pepper
2 Carrots
1 leaf of Kale

Just look at that smile, while I was celebrating the age of 30 with some real good Beet-Juice. Very few things can beat this...

Directions
In juicer/Slow-Juicer, start juicing one ingredient at a time or alternate until everything is done.

– Drink well chilled or directly.

...chewing on my homegrown Kale (page: 32 - 33), next to my lovely houseplant (Philodendron), which has taken over a wall in my bedroom in just 2 years.

Sacred Juice

Psst.. This is a perfect combination of sweet & sour that soothes the taste-buds while boosting the production of enzymes, to help the digestive system do it's job more efficiently; saving tons
of energy along the way.

Ingredients
1 Lemon
3 Apples
4 Carrots

Directions
Peel the ingredients that need peeling, and begin juicing alternately.
– Enjoy well chilled or immediately!
[Add Basil for Zinc & Calcium boost].

Did you know that the highest quality & purest water is found in plants..? Since they get it straight from the source through the roots and is filtered the best way possible (page: 14 - 15). So eating fruits & veggies is literally like eating living water (Fourth Phase: H3O2). Just take a look at a glass of juice.

Just Celery

Why Celery alone?

Well- this is a game-changer in terms of quick recovery, healing of the gut, anti-inflammation, removing the fog in the mind/brain, and much more ...

After watching videos of people healing from various ailments, I had to try it myself for a few months and I've never seen anything like it, my energy levels became a lot more balanced, especially my alertness and focus doubled.

If you'd like to know the reason why celery should not be mixed with other ingredients for best results, look up (Medical Medium), either on social media or on Google. His explanations go even deeper into the details, I'm very grateful for having stumbled upon his invaluable information.

Drinking celery as it is may not be a walk in the park, but after listening to him I had to give it a try and after that, it was a wrap.

The benefits are absolutely incredible. And one of the reasons is that Celery rehydrates the entire body thanks to its above 90% water content that brings a sense of satisfaction, which in turn diminishes cravings almost instantly.

Ingredients
1 Whole Celery plant (400g - 500g)

Directions
Remove the bottom part (and replant it, if you want to): *put it into a glass, add a little water and wait for new roots to appear before putting it in the ground or bucket with soil*. And in less than 3 weeks or so you'll see a brand new celery plant growing.

Wash the stalks thoroughly, chop them into pieces that can fit into your juicer, and begin juicing.

Serve & enjoy immediately, or well chilled.

24

This is a serious part of the journey, it'll turn you into a totally different person. I've come to realize after a lot of research and my own experience that since celery is a Heart Chakra food, it specifically targets emotions. For some reason, you begin to feel way more, it digs deep into emotional wounds leading to surrendering pain/grief/hate/etc ...

...Eventually *letting go* is inevitable (as it continues to pierce layer after layer). Letting go usually is the number one ingredient in life that tends to heal most illnesses in the human body. We often get sick because of stored negative energies for years which unfortunately becomes hereditary in many cases. As a species, we're suffering from traumas more than anything else. Go ahead, take advantage of this plant, and one day you'll testify in your own words.

Health Shot - "Back To Life"

Ingredients
4 large Lemons
100g of fresh Ginger
30g of fresh Turmeric
½ a tsp of Black Pepper
½ a tsp of Cayenne Pepper,
(or 1 fresh chili)
– Alt.: [1 Apple & or 1 cup of Pineapple].

Directions
Peel the lemons (leaving the white part/pith of the inner skin, as it is rich in antioxidants & fiber). Cut them into four pieces each.
Peel the Ginger & Turmeric (not required, if organic) - the skin is very thin.
You're now ready to put the ingredients through the machine, beginning with a few pieces of lemon. Alternate the ingredients,
one at a time.
Pour the juice into a bowl, jar, or any container of your choice. (You get to decide the consistency, add or remove however you wish until you find an elixir that suits your taste). Lastly, add cayenne & black pepper and stir. – (If this is your first time, adding an apple or a few pieces of pineapple makes it even healthier and tastier like a delicious yet powerful juice that keeps the body warm, and increases blood flow).

Facts:
Forget colds, fatigue, inflammations, nausea, headaches, bad breath, joint/back pains, etc.
For better absorption, it is best taken in the morning on an empty stomach, (before your daily routine).

- *Peperine* in Black Pepper is what activates the absorption of curcumin in Turmeric (it is a healthy active compound, which is responsible for the vibrant yellow color).

This is one of my favorite Bumblebees, taking a nap on a dandelion that grew outside of my home. :-)
- Check out more of my little wonderful guests on page: 120 -121.

Rich in:
Vitamin A, C, K, E, Calcium, Magnesium, Potassium, Iron, B Vitamins, etc.

Dandelion Tea

I've always known about dandelion being a powerful natural medicine alongside other great herbs that grow freely here and there such as chamomile, but for some reason I never saw myself using it, plus that I had certain beliefs about it, as you may know - it is perceived as an annoying weed by most people. But I finally gave it a go, and I was surprised, it tastes really good and has a pleasant aroma.
I added a little bit of fresh ginger, turmeric, vanilla powder, and cinnamon. Yes, it can definitely be enjoyed as is in hot water or even in juices & smoothies. Also leaves and even roots are used as remedies - (remember to do your own research for more mind blowing health benefits).

Dandelion is specifically a liver detoxifying plant with a myriad other health benefits similar to those of many super-foods of nature.

After just 1 week I noticed my stamina had doubled especially when on my bicycle for about an hour, there was no sign of tiredness, though I had been up for over 20 hours mostly editing this book.

Dandelion tea is a perfect drink in the morning before or during breakfast. So next time you see them, pick as many as you can, and freeze or dry them for later use. They're beautiful, free of charge, and a gift from nature to all of us for healing.

This little plant can help people with diabetes, arthritis, heart problems, and many other health issues; big and small.

Ingredients

3 medium Carrots
3 medium Oranges
2 medium red Apples
1 inch of fresh Turmeric
2 inches of fresh Ginger

– For the multicolor art:
¼ cup of frozen Blueberries
⅓ cup of sliced & frozen Mango

Directions

In a juicer, make juice out of the oranges, apples, turmeric & ginger.
In a blender, mix the juice with mango, and put it aside.
Make carrot juice, and put it aside.
Blend the blueberries, add some water if too frozen.
Now pour each ingredient into a bottle or jar, one at a time, and watch as it all slowly turns into a colorful delicious beverage.

@ECO_AIR_US

2015   2022

I enjoyed this magnificent potion while celebrating the New Year of 2022, and a 7-year cycle since my first real smoothie journey that I embarked on back in 2015 for a whole year of up to 90% smoothies. My life hasn't been the same ever since.

Green Smoothie w/ Homegrown Kale

Ingredients

2 large ripe Bananas
4 - 6 leaves of Kale
A handful of Mint leaves
1 cup of Coconut Water (or any liquid)

Directions

Put all the ingredients in a blender, and mix until you're satisfied with the consistency. – Enjoy immediately or well chilled!

I had to share this simple recipe for no reason other than the fact that I was successful in growing my own Kale from scratch after many attempts for a few years. I'm so proud because I did it on my porch in a small pallet collar, (see page: 96 - 97).

Kale is considered a superfood:
which contains fiber, antioxidants, calcium, vitamins C and K, iron, and a wide range of other nutrients. Antioxidants help the body remove unwanted toxins, making it the perfect choice when planning to do a thorough cleanse or detox.

All greens have Chlorophyll, and its benefits are:
- Cancer prevention.
- Healing wounds.
- Skin care and acne treatment.
- Weight loss.
- Controlling body odor.
- Relieving constipation and gas.
- Boosting energy.

Smooth Mango

"I'm adding this one because sometimes you don't have more than one or two
ingredients available, and just want to keep it simple and it's OK. Mangoes &
Bananas are very healthy anyhow."
(If you don't have fresh mangoes, frozen ones work perfectly as well).

– Fun facts about Mango: It is great for hair and skin thanks to its rich content of
Retinol (vitamin A), it helps reduce blood sugar levels, and it also lowers levels
of fats in the blood.

Ingredients

2 cups of fresh Mango, (1 & ½)
2 medium extra ripe Bananas
- (Optional: a bit of ice or water)

Directions

Peel the mango, separate the flesh from the core/
pit, chop the edible part into small pieces, and put
them in a blender.
Then peel the banana, add it to the mix as well,
and blend into a smooth and nice beverage - (you
decide the thickness).

Enjoy chilled or straight away.

- (It can be refrigerated for up to 3 days *well-
sealed*).

Just:

MANGO
&
BANANA

Choco Galia Love

Ingredients

½ of an Avocado
1 tsp of Raw Cacao
½ of a Galia Melon
1 large ripe Banana
Nuts/Seeds (for decor)

Directions

Peel the banana and make a smoothie using a blender -
(Optional: add some coconut milk or any plant-based milk of your choice, if too thick).
Add a teaspoon of raw cacao to the mix.
Now gently pour the smoothie into a bowl and begin filling it up with the rest of the
ingredients, starting with pieces or scoops of the Galia melon in the center using a spoon,
and then go ahead with the rest of the magical work of decorating.

Definitely something for the lovers of fast, but healthy meals.
It couldn't get any simpler to get a bunch of vitamins, essential natural fats, and antioxidants in a single exquisite and beautiful bowl of love.
This can be eaten as a power breakfast or anytime really, I mean who's out here checking the time – right..?

Facts about Galia melon: it is rich in antioxidants, which can help reduce the risk of serious health conditions like cancer, diabetes, stroke, and heart disease. Galia melon is also an excellent source of: Potassium.

I often say that my favorite fruit is Mango & Avocado, but really if I had to choose between those & Galia Melon, it'd be one serious battle. There's something about Galia that makes my digestive system feel like I did as a baby. Nothing beats that sensation! — (Yes Avocado is indeed a fruit), isn't that something?

Eddy Coleson

Milky Way

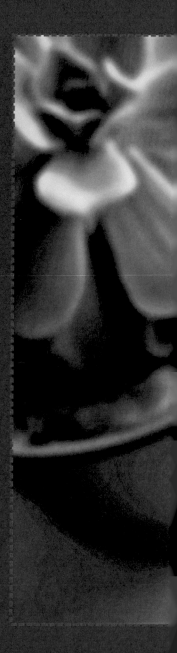

Ingredients
1 large Banana
⅓ tsp of Cinnamon
½ a cup of Oat Milk
1 Tsp of Peanut Butter

Directions
Mix all the ingredients in a blender,
(if you don't have peanuts or peanut butter,
you can use any other kind of nut), you can
even use apple juice in the place of oat milk for
smoother digestion & a boost in vitamins.

The purpose of this elixir is to boost your energy levels
especially when you have no time to make a meal. It is
rich in protein, making it perfect when you're about to
work out, or right after for a quick recovery.

Cinnamon: has antiviral, antibacterial and anti-fungal properties that help reduce respiratory diseases and seasonal infections, while lowering blood sugar along the way.

Peanut butter: contains omega-6. This fatty acid lowers bad (LDL) cholesterol, and increases protective (HDL) cholesterol. In addition, peanuts are a natural source of arginine, an amino acid that may prevent heart and vascular diseases by promoting good blood vessel function.

The Green Vortex

Ingredients

½ a small Lime
2 medium ripe Bananas
1 cup of Spinach (60g / 1 huge handful)
1 cup of Water / Ice (or any plant-based liquid)

Directions

Peel the Bananas, then put them in a blender together with all the other ingredients, and turn it on until you see a smooth green substance without any chunks in it.
− You can enjoy it cold, or right away.

Facts about Spinach:
It is great for hair & skin thanks to folate, vitamins A, C & E.
You've also heard about or even seen movies about Popeye and how strong he is because he's always eating spinach. There's something to it, as it contains significant amounts of Calcium which is the foundation of what the skeleton/bones are made of. Take great care of the bones, they're literally the pillars of the temple that is YOU.

- Book: *"Spiritual Surgery"* - by Eddy Coleson

Compassion

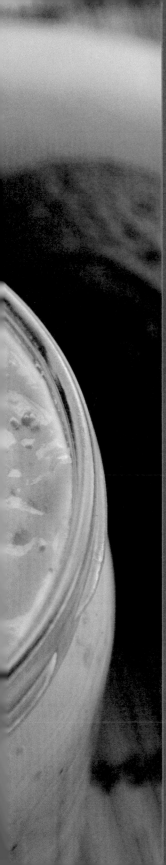

Ingredients

½ a cup of Mango
1 medium Avocado
1 large ripe Banana
1 tsp of Chia Seeds
A handful of Mint leaves
3 - 4 Sea Buckthorn Berries

Directions

Peel what needs peeling, then put all the ingredients in a blender, and mix until it becomes a thick creamy substance. (If too thick for your taste, add some liquid of your choice, preferably apple juice).

Did you know that a few Sea Buckthorn Berries have more vitamin C than a whole Orange or Lemon?
It is one among the super-foods of nature with health benefits such as:

- Treat stomach or intestinal problems.
- Improve blood pressure or blood cholesterol.
- Prevent or manage blood vessel or heart disease.
- Complement cancer treatment.
- Boost immunity and prevent infections.
- Treat obesity.
- Improve symptoms of cirrhosis.
- Treat vaginal dryness.
- Improve eyesight or dry eyes.

Tempeh Salad - (with Coco Wraps)

Ingredients

Coconut Wraps
1 cup of Cashews
1 cup of Tempeh
1/2 a Cucumber
1 Medium Avocado
1/2 cup of Plum Tomatoes
1 cup of Asparagus
1/2 a red Onion
2 cloves of Garlic
1/2 a long Sweet Pepper
1/2 a yellow Pepper
1/3 cup of Chanterelle
1/3 tsp of Cayenne Pepper
1 Tbsp of Soy Sauce, (or Coconut Aminos)
1 Tbsp of Extra Virgin Coconut Oil
1 large Carrot, (shredded)
A handful of green Lentil Sprouts
1/3 tsp of Oregano
1 Tbsp of Lemon Juice
1/2 cup of Coconut Milk
1/2 a tsp of Sesame Seeds (for decoration)
A pinch of pink Himalayan Salt
1/2 a Chili (Optional)

Dressing / Sauce:

Soak Cashews a bit ahead of time for easier blending later when making the sauce/dressing. When the cooking is almost ready put the cashews, a thumb-sized piece of onion, 2 cloves of garlic, a teaspoon of soy sauce (or coconut aminos), a pinch of Himalayan salt, 1/2 a tsp of lemon juice, an inch of chili, and 1/2 an inch of fresh ginger in a blender. Add the coconut milk gradually and decide the preferred consistency as you go.

Directions

Start by boiling the asparagus in water for up to 5 minutes. In the meantime, fry the tempeh in a little bit of coconut oil and add some salt, cayenne pepper, and soy sauce (or coconut aminos) for that little extra taste. Then put it aside when ready.

Fry the asparagus as well just a bit or until you're satisfied with the result. (Btw- there's no special reason for frying each ingredient individually, it just looks better later when serving, in my opinion).

Now fry the red onion, yellow peppers, sprinkle some lemon juice, then add the Chanterelle at the last minute (they're very sensitive). And of course, most of the veggies can be eaten raw, for those who want to do so.

Set up an eye-catching plate (see image for inspiration), then last but not least the best part is stuffing the coconut wraps with a little bit of everything on the menu and then rolling them. – Congratulations!!

Spring Rolls w/ Baked Sweet Potato

Ingredients

1 medium Sweet Potato
2 Rice rolls
1 medium Avocado
1/2 of a long sweet Pepper
1/3 of a red Onion
2 cloves of Garlic
1 small Lime
2 leaves of Lettuce
1 cup of Coconut Milk
A pinch of Cayenne Pepper
1 tsp of Soy Sauce,
(or Coconut Aminos)
A handful of Cilantro & Basil
1 tsp of Sesame Seeds
1 cup of Cashews
1/2 an inch of Chili (Optional)

Directions

Soak the cashews in warm water. Meanwhile, preheat the oven on max (250°C / 482°F) and bring it back to half the temperature after 5 minutes.

In the meantime, chop the sweet potato as you would French fries but a bit thicker pieces, then cook in boiling water and remove from the stove pouring out the water to avoid getting them soft/mushy – (4 to 5 minutes in boiling water on maximum heat is usually enough).

Transfer the sweet potatoes to a baking tray, brush them with some coconut oil, and put them in the oven for up to 10 minutes until they get
a nice golden color.

Soak the rice rolls one at a time not longer than 5 seconds in lukewarm water, then carefully lay it on a flat surface and start filling it up starting with lettuce to prevent poking holes in it (see instructions on the original packaging). Continue adding the rest of your ingredients, then fold the sheet to create a nice and neat roll. – Enjoy!

- Dressing / Sauce:

In a blender add 1/3 of a red onion, a handful of cilantro & basil, 2 cloves of garlic, 1 tsp of sesame seeds, 1 cup of soaked cashews, 1 tsp of soy sauce (or coconut aminos), 1 tsp of lime juice, a pinch of cayenne pepper, then (optional) for some extra heat add a piece of chili, lastly add the coconut milk gradually to your liking as you blend everything together.

- [No rice sheets? No problems, any kind of wraps would work well].

Heaven in a Wrap

Ingredients

Cinnamon flavored Coconut Wraps
1 medium Sweet Potato
1 large Carrot, (shredded)
1/2 a tsp of Lemon Juice
A handful of fresh Basil & Cilantro
Furikake/Sesame/Pumpkin Seeds
Green Lentil Sprouts
(Any other leafy greens: optional)
Pink Himalayan Salt (optional)
1 Tbsp of Extra Virgin Coconut Oil
1/3 of a red Pepper
1/4 of red Onion
1 medium Avocado

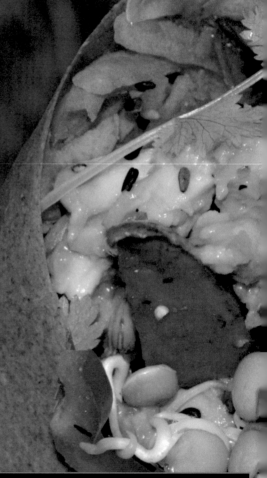

Directions

Slice the sweet potato into long and nice pieces. Boil in a pot for about 4 minutes (keep the skin on, it has amazing health benefits among them powerful antioxidants). Heat up the oven, prepare a baking tray with coconut oil on it.

Transfer the sweet potato to the tray, make sure every piece is oiled, and then put it in the oven until a nice golden color appears. (You can also bake the sweet potato directly without having to cook it first).

Once the sweet potato is ready, you can then start laying the ingredients on a wrap however you like, then garnish with seeds & herbs – (see images for inspiration).

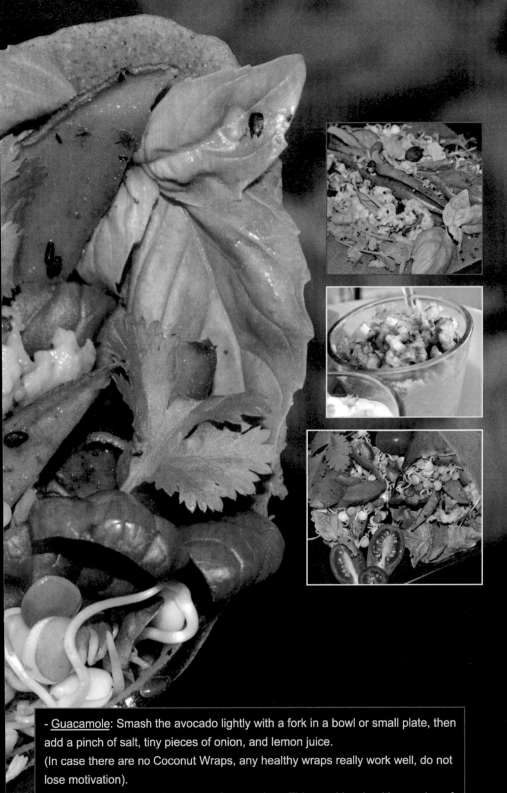

- <u>Guacamole</u>: Smash the avocado lightly with a fork in a bowl or small plate, then add a pinch of salt, tiny pieces of onion, and lemon juice.

(In case there are no Coconut Wraps, any healthy wraps really work well, do not lose motivation).

This is a wonderful treat, that's perfect anytime. This meal is a healthy version of fast-food.

Nori Roll

– Stuffing:
Alfalfa sprouts, pea sprouts, avocado, cherry tomatoes, spinach, arugula,
swiss chard, portobello mushrooms, green & yellow peppers, sun-dried
tomatoes, furikake, cilantro, basil, a small chili
is optional & tofu lightly fried in extra virgin coconut oil (w/ onion, cayenne,
fresh ginger, soy sauce or coconut aminos & garlic).

Apart from having way more Calcium than milk, Nori also
has almost all of the most important essential Vitamins
that the body needs. And thanks to its rich content of
vitamin C, the bioavailability of its abundant
iron content is increased.

– <u>Sauce/Dip</u>:

1/2 a cup of soaked cashews (in 1/2 a cup of coconut - or oat milk).
Blend with 1/4 of a red bell pepper, 1/4 of a yellow bell pepper, 1/3
of a medium red onion, 1 clove of garlic, a pinch of cayenne
pepper, a pinch of Himalayan pink salt, a handful of cilantro &
basil, 1/2 a tsp of furikake: (sesame seeds, etc.)

Mostly Homegrown Salad

Chickpea Dressing (In a blender):
1 & 1/2 cup of chickpeas, 2 cloves of garlic, 1/3 of a red onion,
a pinch of Himalayan pink salt, 1/2 cup of coconut milk, 1 tsp of lemon
juice, 1/2 a chili, a handful of cilantro & basil.

Ingredients

- 1/2 a Cucumber
- A handful of Cilantro
- A handful of Basil
- Yellow Cherry Tomatoes
- A few leaves of Kale
- 1 small Chili
- 1/2 a red Bell Pepper
- 1 cup of green Lentil-Sprouts
- 1/3 of a red Onion
- 2 cloves of Garlic
- 1/2 a tsp of Lemon-Juice
- A few Broccoli Leaves
- 1/2 a cup of Corn Kernels
- 1 tsp of Sesame Seeds
- a pinch of pink Himalayan Salt
- 1 cup of Chickpeas

Directions

In this one, there's no need to cook anything except for the corn kernels (if you must). The only processing needed is the chickpea dressing. The rest only needs to be chopped and put nicely on a plate – (see image).

I am including this recipe as another inspiration, not only to encourage eating more greens, which is amazing for the body in terms of cleansing and absorbing vitamins and minerals. But also because I believe it's very important for the future of humanity to know what's in the food, even more so when we grow it ourselves regardless of the scale. If each one of us grew something we'd eradicate a lot of confusion and many health issues in the world.

This planet that we've been gifted is made of greenery and depends on just that, and so do we. So if we want to see life continue naturally, we're going to have to contribute to it on a continuous basis by planting more seeds tirelessly. Our presence alone here is taking from nature, this is why cherishing the environment by giving back through planting seeds is paramount.

Smoky Almond Sauce

Ingredients

A handful of roasted Almonds
1/4 of a red Bell Pepper
1/4 of a yellow Bell Pepper
A slice of red Onion
1 clove of Garlic
1/2 a cup of Water
1/2 inch of fresh Ginger
A pinch of pink Himalayan Salt
A handful of Cilantro & Basil
1/3 a tsp of Extra Virgin Coconut Oil
1/2 a tsp of Soy Sauce, (or Coconut Aminos)
A small piece of Chili, or a pinch of Cayenne Pepper

Directions

Mix all the ingredients together at once, or a few at a time using a blender.
You're looking for a smooth and thick substance.

You can always add or subtract ingredients to fit your taste. The
consistency is all up to you.

Enjoy this delicious dressing with seed crackers. See page: 90.

The roasted Almonds give any meal a barbecue sauce taste. It goes well
with absolutely anything.
this here is a salad with curried minced tofu.

Green Lentil Sprouts

Take 3 full tablespoons of lentils, put them in a container/jar, add water and let them soak (once) overnight in a dark space.

On the 2nd day, pour the water out and rinse the lentils thoroughly. Repeat this process each day until little sprouts begin to appear. They can be eaten early as sprouts or even when they begin to grow little long grass-like plants. They make salads look very appetizing and appealing as seen in many of the recipes throughout the book.

You'll need:

A sprouting jar or simply a jar. Any type of container works well.

The most important is that you must drain the water.

(Rinse multiple times per day if it's in the summertime to avoid dehydration).

I use a kind of sprouting box/tray.

Almost any whole raw grains, and or seeds can be sprouted.

Day 1 through 6

See page: 44

[These are called microgreens, and according to studies it is an important part of the future in terms of healthy nutrition]. It is convenient both for farms and home, plus it's pretty fun and easy to do for all ages.

Spicy Cashew Dip

Soak the Cashews (in water: 1 cup), overnight.

Ingredients

1 cup of Cashews
1/3 of a red Onion
1 clove of Garlic
1 small Chili
A pinch of Cayenne Pepper
1/2 a tsp of Curry
A handful of Cilantro & Basil
A pinch of pink Himalayan Salt
1/4 of yellow & red Pepper
1/4 of a long Sweet Pepper
1/2 a tsp of Panang Gai,
 (Thai Mixed Spices)

Directions

In a blender, mix all the ingredients together into a smooth creamy sauce or until you get a desired consistency.
Enjoy in a coco wrap with veggies or on a seed cracker: (See page: 90 & 94).

Moringa oleifera is **rich in antioxidants like beta-carotene**. These antioxidants help protect against heart disease, cancer, immune system deficiency, and inflammatory conditions, – on top of Aminos Acids & B Vitamins.

In this Moringa flavored coconut wrap there's so much goodies, and it satisfies both the belly and taste buds in terms of sweet & salt from natural sources.

It literally takes two palms to handle it. Of course one can choose how much and or what to fill it up with, as long as it's healthy and fresh - right?

Tacos w/ Homegrown Cherry Tomatoes

Ingredients

½ a cup of sliced Tofu
½ a medium Avocado
A handful of Cilantro & Basil
A handful of Pea-Shoots
½ a medium Red Onion
2 cloves of Garlic
A few Cherry Tomatoes
Sesame Seeds or Furikake
1 inch of fresh Ginger
½ a tsp of Lemon Juice
½ a red & yellow sweet Pepper
A pinch of Pink Himalayan salt
1 Tbsp of Extra Virgin Coconut Oil
1 Tbsp of Soy Sauce or Coconut Aminos
Tortilla Wraps & Tortilla Chips

Directions

Put a frying pan on a stove, add coconut oil, then fry the tofu until you get a nice bronze color. Successively add onion, garlic, ginger, peppers, salt, soy sauce, (or coconut aminos), lemon juice, and continue for about 4 more minutes (on medium heat towards the end).

Sprinkle some sesame seeds or furikake, and serve in a tortilla or any wrap of your choice garnished with pea shootings or sprouts.

Dressing (in a blender):

½ a cup of Cashews, (Soaked)
½ a medium red & yellow Peppers
1 clove of Garlic
½ a cup of Oat Milk
3 - 4 Cherry Tomatoes
A pinch of pink Himalayan Salt
A pinch of Cayenne Pepper
Some Basil & Cilantro

- See the amazing tomatoes on the next page.

61

After harvesting my late November cherry tomatoes, I had to make something special, delicious and memorable. As you may have noticed I love simple but tasty dressings. The taste of the dressing/sauce was really amazing thanks to the sweetness of my homegrown tomatoes. It was better than I expected.

This here was one of the most special and exciting moments for me in the year 2021, these beauties are so sweet it's almost unreal. They grew on their own in a mini raised bed pallet collar where I throw leftover veggies, etc... I just kept watering the soil whenever it seemed dry. Would you believe that I harvested them in the middle of November..? (I live in the northern hemisphere).

Miso Soup – (Pineapple Flavor)

Ingredients

1 cup of sliced/cubed Tofu
1 cup of sliced sweet potato
1/2 a cup of Wakame
1/2 a red Onion
1 small (chopped) Chili
A handful of Basil & Cilantro
2 Tbsp of Extra Virgin Coconut Oil
3 cloves of Garlic
1 inch of fresh Ginger
2 sheets of Nori/Seaweed
1 Tbsp of Furikake/Sesame Seeds
1/2 a tsp of Cayenne Pepper
1/2 a tsp of pink Himalayan Salt
4 - 5 cups of Water
1/2 a Red Bell Pepper
1 tsp of Miso Paste
1 Tbsp of Soy Sauce
1/2 a cup of thick Coconut Milk
1 Tbsp of pineapple flavored spice,
(or 8 - 10 Tbsp of Pineapple Juice)

- If the sweet potato is organic, do not peel it, the skin has antioxidants and is rich in fiber.

Dare re-mix this recipe by adding cooked red lentils instead of seaweed / tofu - (see images below):

Directions

Begin by boiling wakame and nori/seaweed in water for about 5 minutes, while on the side in a frying pan fry onions, garlic, bell pepper, cayenne pepper, and chili - (an ingredient at a time one after the other).

in a different pot, boil sweet potato (make sure it doesn't get too soft), 5 minutes on medium heat is usually enough.

On medium heat add tofu to the frying pan, stir a bit and then add soy sauce, fresh ginger, furikake/sesame seeds, basil & cilantro. Lastly, add pineapple-flavored spice (or pineapple juice). Stir until you get a beautiful color and a pleasing aroma.

Take a little bit of water from the seaweed and pour it into the frying pan, then add miso paste. Stir well while adding coconut milk.

[To make sweet potato tastier, fry it real quick in a bit of coconut oil, or even better bake it in the oven slightly oiled].

You're now ready to merge everything together into a nice and delicious soup, let it simmer on low heat for a few minutes all together in the same pot, (you can also keep everything separated if you want to).

Serve warm and garnish with some furikake, cilantro & basil.

– Enjoy!

Curried Miso w/ Rice Noodles

Boil 4 - 5 cups of water in a pot, then add the nori sheets and wakame in it. Let it simmer for 5 minutes on low heat.

Fill up a different pot with water to the middle, put it on the stove, and once it begins to boil, add the minced tofu. Let it cook for 5 minutes on medium heat.

Ingredients

1 cup of minced Tofu
1 cup of Tomato sauce/paste
2 Tbsp of Extra Virgin Coconut Oil
1/2 cup of Wakame
1/2 a red Onion
3 cloves of Garlic
1 inch of fresh Ginger
2 sheets of Nori/Seaweed
1 Tbsp of Furikake/Sesame Seeds
1/2 a tsp of Cayenne Pepper
A pinch of pink Himalayan Salt
4 - 5 cups of Water
1/2 a red Bell Pepper
1 cup of Rice noodles
1 tsp of Miso paste
1 Tbsp of Soy Sauce, (or coconut aminos)
Oregano/Herbs (for decor)
Green Lentil Sprouts

Directions

Heat up the coconut oil on medium heat in a frying pan, then begin to chop the onion, garlic, bell pepper, chili, and ginger, then fry all these in a frying pan one after the other. Spice it up with cayenne pepper & a pinch of pink Himalayan salt.

Once the minced tofu is ready, drain the water and then transfer it to the fried ingredients and stir until everything begins to smell great. Add the tomato sauce/paste, soy sauce (or coconut aminos), miso paste, furikake/sesame seeds (ground). Then add some water to avoid chunks.

You can now go ahead and boil water for the noodles (they're cooked just like spaghetti, except they're a bit more sensitive).

In the meantime, transfer the water with wakame & nori in it, to the frying pan where you have minced tofu and all that. Stir everything together, it should be a soup-like consistency. When the noodles are ready, drain the water. Serve the soup in a bowl, add the noodles to it, then sprinkle some herbs/seeds on top for the fun of it.

Dressing

<u>In a blender:</u>
1/2 cup of Cashews & Almonds (soaked), a handful of fresh Basil
& Parsley, 1/4 tsp of Thyme, 1/4 tsp of Oregano, 1/3 tsp of Cumin, 1/4 tsp of
Cayenne Pepper, 1/3 tsp of Chili, 1 tsp of Sesame Seeds, a little pink Himalayan Salt,
1 inch of fresh Ginger, 1/5 of a red Onion, 1 clove of Garlic, 1/4 tsp of Turmeric, 1/2 a
tsp of Lemon Juice, 1/2 a yellow Bell Pepper & 1/5 cup of Coconut Milk.

Burger w/ Raw Portobello

It doesn't necessarily have to be mushrooms, you can use other things such as wraps, etc.

Directions

Burger: 1 cup (≈ 200g) of cooked minced soy, drain and add 1/2 tsp of Basil, 1/2 tsp of Parsley, 1/3 tsp of Thyme, 1/4 tsp of Oregano, 1/2 tsp Cumin, 1/3 tsp of Cayenne, 1/2 tsp of Chili, 1/4 tsp of pink Himalayan Salt, 1/3 tsp of Turmeric, 5 cloves of Garlic, 1/2 a red Onion, 1 Tbsp of Lemon Juice, 1 Tbsp of Soy Sauce (or Coconut Aminos), 1 Tbsp of Miso Paste, 2 to 2,5 Tbsp of [Vegan] Butter. 1 to 1,5 cups Soaked Oats as binding material. *Stir well, shape and put into an oven*.

IN PREHEATED OVEN FOR 30 - 40 MINUTES ON 175°C, (347°F).

Coco Vibes Pasta

This is a balanced, nutritious, and satisfying meal, with enough carbohydrates to fuel the body especially on an active day, which is also perfect before (or after a workout).
This is perfect to eat as a 'one meal' for the day, preferably as lunch.

Ingredients

2 cups of Durum wheat pasta
(Multicolored: Optional)
1 cup of smoked Tofu
2 - 3 Tbsp of Coconut Cream
1 cup of Tomato paste/sauce
2 Tbsp of Virgin Coconut Oil
A pinch of pink Himalayan Salt
1/2 a tsp of Curry
1/2 a Red Onion
4 cloves of Garlic
1/3 tsp of Black Pepper
A pinch of Cayenne Pepper
1/3 cup of Sun-dried Tomatoes
A handful of Basil
1/2 a Red Bell Pepper
1 Tbsp of Lime Juice, (Optional)

Directions

Boil water in a cooking pot (for the pasta). Add a little salt to it & 1/2 a tsp of coconut oil to prevent the pasta from sticking to each other.

Fry onion, garlic, bell pepper, a pinch of salt in coconut oil. Then add slices of tofu, black pepper & curry.

In the meantime, you can now add pasta to the boiled water for the next 4 - 5 minutes on medium heat – (avoid overcooking).

Back to the sauce. As you smell a heavenly aroma filling the room, add tomato paste/sauce, coconut cream, and continue stirring on medium heat. Turn the stove off and wait for the pasta.

Check on the pasta, pour the water out, then transfer it to the pan where you have the sauce and mix everything together.

Lastly, throw in some fresh basil leaves & pieces of dried tomato. Garnish with some cherry tomatoes and slices of cucumber.

– Enjoy warm, and if you want a perfect salad with essential fats and even more protein, add some avocado slices to it, and why not some (lime juice: optional). Yum, thank me later. :-)

Nature's Snacks

Not to promote mono meals, but the more and more fresh foods you eat, you're going to realize that not only is the amount of food you need during the day less but also the cravings will go from wanting something to provide you with a false sense of comfort, to something that contributes to the well-being you're already building up.

So don't be shy, grab some grapes, or why not in combination with oranges, and treat yourself. They're very rich in vitamins, liquid, antioxidants, they also have the capacity to lower blood sugar, and prevent chronic diseases.

Throw a few pieces into your water while you're at it, it helps the body absorb it more efficiently.

It's amazing what a small bowl of fruit can do for the intestines, once the gut has finally learned how to extract and process nutrients properly. We tend to eat more due to poor absorption, (unnatural foods lacking enough nutrients).
Satiety is not the result of the amount of food we intake, it is rather determined by how nutrient-dense the food is. Thus - quality is always better than quantity!

Grapes are the most healing little things, their seeds are full of flavonoids which are great for detoxification, and also contain melatonin which is great for the brain and heart health. Melatonin is a powerful antioxidant, as well as a natural antidepressant produced by the Pineal Gland in the brain, which is also responsible for regulating sleep cycles: (Circadian Rhythm).

Breakfast for Champions

Never microwave oatmeal!

It should be soaked, and cooked in at least three times the amount of water as that of the oatmeal — (i.e: 1 cup of oatmeal in 3 cups of water).

— <u>Fun facts</u>:

Oatmeal reduces the 'bad' LDL cholesterol, and increases the 'good' HDL cholesterol levels.

It also lowers blood sugar levels, and is a powerful colon cleanser.

Some granola? (D.I.Y on page: 92 - 93).

Ingredients
1 & 1/2 cups of Soaked Oats, (overnight)
3 cups of Coconut Milk
1 tsp of Extra Virgin Coconut Oil
A pinch of Vanilla powder
1 cup of frozen berries of your choice: (Mango,
Strawberry, Blackberry, Blueberry, Raspberry)
1 ripe Kiwi
Buckthorn Berries
1/2 ripe Banana
1 Tbsp of chopped Sun-dried Dates
2 Tbsp of Granola, (optional)
A few drops of Agave/Syrup, (for the sweet tooth)
1 Tbsp of Peanut Butter,
(for extra protein & healthy fats)

Directions
Boil water in a saucepan, and then put the soaked
oats in it for about 4 to 5 minutes.

Stir every now and then.
Add some coconut milk and regulate the
consistency to your liking.
Add coconut oil, then vanilla, and continue stirring
on medium heat.

Put it aside, (it shouldn't be chunky or too thick.
The consistency must appear similar to that of a
smoothie).

Serve warm with berries, sliced banana, some
kiwi pieces, dried fruit as decoration and as a
highly nutritious complement simultaneously.

Timeless Chia Pudding

This one is for the fun of it. I decorated it to make those who have never heard of Chia Seeds remember it every time they hear or see it because it is one of the most powerful superfoods in nature.

It has all 9 essential amino acids, making it a reliable source of protein, and also heart-healthy omega 3 fatty acids & 6. It is like eating meat, seaweed, and fish all at once. This is for anyone working on reducing their consumption of animal products, which of course is also great for our environment in the long run.

- In this recipe, you find Hemp Seeds that contain Omega 9, which is great for brain health among other things.

Ingredients

3 - 4 Tbsp of Chia Seeds
2 cups of Coconut Milk / (any liquid)
Vanilla or Cinnamon
1 Tbsp of Raw Agave / syrup
Some Nuts/Seeds/Fruit/Berries/etc.

Directions

All you need is to soak the chia seeds in your preferred liquid for a while (stir/beat/whisk for a minute to make sure it is well mixed).

Let sit for at least 30 minutes to an hour - (overnight is even better). – *Chia Seeds absorb the liquid and swell over time, turning into a jelly-like substance*.

When ready, transfer the mass to a glass/bowl (decorate as you wish, find inspiration from the images provided for you). – Enjoy!

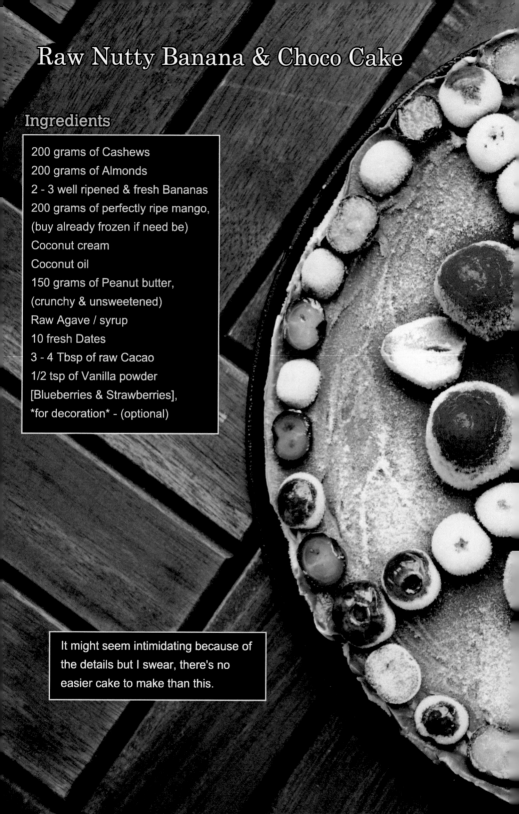

Raw Nutty Banana & Choco Cake

Ingredients

200 grams of Cashews
200 grams of Almonds
2 - 3 well ripened & fresh Bananas
200 grams of perfectly ripe mango,
(buy already frozen if need be)
Coconut cream
Coconut oil
150 grams of Peanut butter,
(crunchy & unsweetened)
Raw Agave / syrup
10 fresh Dates
3 - 4 Tbsp of raw Cacao
1/2 tsp of Vanilla powder
[Blueberries & Strawberries],
for decoration - (optional)

It might seem intimidating because of
the details but I swear, there's no
easier cake to make than this.

Directions

<u>Bottom layer</u>:

a. - Crush the almonds in a blender (even better in a food processor, if available). *It doesn't have to be too finely crushed*.

b. - Now put the crushed almonds in a bowl, add 2 full table spoons of raw agave and knead until it turns into a dough (shouldn't be sticky)! Add just 100 grams of the peanut butter and keep kneading until you get a nice clay looking mass.

c. - Place that in a round form (with parchment paper at the bottom), and spread evenly, then put it in the freezer.

<u>Middle layer</u>:

a. - Blend the cashews alone in a clean & dry blender/food processor to the point where you achieve a butter like consistency (It can take some time when using a blender depending on the power, just keep mixing). *This is key & the most important part*.

b. - When the cashew is ready throw in the bananas, mango, coconut oil, dates, 2 table spoons of raw agave, about 1/2 a teaspoon of vanilla powder. (You can add one or a few things at a time if you like, the most important thing is that the final result of the mix becomes so smooth looking and fine as a smoothie, *but a pretty thick one*; it should be like a thick paste)!

c. - Get the bottom layer out of the freezer and add the now ready middle layer, even it out as well as possible and put it back in the freezer (1 - 2 hours for the best consistency).

Yay, finally the fastest & easiest part:

Top layer: (you can begin with this layer right before the 2 hours are over:
a. - Mix the following together:
50 grams of the remaining peanut butter (not necessary unless you really love peanut butter.. Without it this layer is then just a thin chocolate cover which can be kinda boring), raw cacao, 2 - 3 Tbsp of liquefied coconut oil (not very practical if the oil is too hard/solid), 2 - 3 Tbsp of raw agave, between 2 - 4 Tbsp of coconut cream (you decide how creamy you want it). Now blend until very fine and fairly thick.
b. - Last but not least get the frozen layers out of the freezer and spread the final layer on top. (Decorate the cake after about 15 minutes in the freezer).
— ..Congratulations, you're now done. Freeze for at least 6 - 8 hours.
I'd leave it until the next day. - Enjoy!!

Ingredients

1 cup of frozen Blueberries.
2 cups of soaked Cashews.
1 Tbsp of Extra Virgin Coconut Oil.
½ a tsp of ground Vanilla.
1 cup of raw Almonds.
10 - 12 fresh pitted Dates.
A Muffin or Cupcake tray.
- Optional: (Strawberries/Raspberries/etc. for decoration).

Directions

Crust / Bottom: Crush almonds using a high-speed blender or food processor, for a few seconds (avoid turning them into flour, you want a crunchy consistency). Add 5 - 7 pitted dates (this is the binding material) and continue crushing for a few more seconds, then take the mix out of the machine using a spoon or a spatula, and mold it with your hands to even out the consistency.

Put muffin liners in the tray, then start filling them with the almond crust (this is the bottom layer). You decide how thick it should be. When you're done, put the tray in the freezer while working on the next layer.

Cream: Rinse & dry your blender, then put the soaked cashews in it (drained). Now unlike the crust, this should be mixed until there are absolutely no chunks left (very important because this part is the equivalent of cream in conventional ice cream). Once you achieve a chunk-free substance that looks like wet powder/flour, add the blueberries, 5 dates, and blend/mix until you see a beautiful purple and really thick smoothie-like consistency.

Now add vanilla, coconut oil, and blend/mix for the last time.

Take the muffin tray out of the freezer and start filling it up with the purple beauty carefully using a spoon (evenly). Once you're satisfied with your work of art, tap the tray gently against the table/counter to even the substances out, then decorate as you wish - (see images for inspiration). And finally put the muffin tray back into the freezer overnight to be enjoyed the next day.

Blueberry Nice Cream Cupcakes

<< Once you've mastered this process, you'll be able to choose any other kind of berries or even create layers with different colors and have lots of fun. The most important is the consistency of the creamy part. >>

With Mango & Lime.

Psst.. Try the cashew cream on a pie, with or without blueberries - (See next page for inspiration).

Mini Oat Muffin Pies

Ingredients

150g - 200g of ground Oats (into fine flour)
1 & ½ red Apples
A handful of Blueberries
1 tsp of ground Cinnamon
1 Tbsp of raw Agave / syrup
A pinch of Himalayan pink salt
½ a tsp of ground Vanilla
1 & ½ Tbsp of Extra Virgin Coconut Oil
3 - 5 Tbsp of cold Water
1 tsp of Ginger Juice
2 Tbsp of Lemon Juice

Directions

Filling (Cooked Apple Slices):
Peel (optional), 1 & 1/2 apples, slice them into tiny pieces, and cook them in boiling water for 5 minutes (not to be too soft).
Add 1 tsp of cinnamon, 1 tsp of ginger juice / extract, 2 Tbsp of lemon juice (or Apple Cider Vinegar, *which I personally no longer use due to its negative effects on the absorption of calcium in the body*), 1 Tbsp of raw agave / syrup, and stir a little bit. When ready empty the water, put it on the side and continue to the next task.
Crust: Grind the oats into flour. Transfer it to a bowl, add a pinch of Himalayan pink salt, and 1/2 a tsp of ground vanilla.
Whilst stirring, add extra virgin coconut oil (in liquid form), you can heat it up real quick.
Continue stirring with a spoon or spatula, add a bit of cold water at a time (not more than a few tablespoons).
Then add 2 tsp of raw agave syrup, and keep going (you're looking for a clay-like substance that is sticky & does not disintegrate). It should be a nice and firm dough!
When you're satisfied with the result, put muffin liners in a muffin tray (I double the liners to make sure they're firm all the way). Fill them up with a significantly thin layer of the dough, leaving enough space in the middle for the rest of the ingredients.
Put the tray in the oven for about 8 to 10 minutes on 302°F (150°C).
Lastly, take the tray out and fill the muffin liners with the apple pieces and blueberries, then put the tray back in the oven for another 10 minutes on medium heat. – *It's a good idea to cover them the first 5 minutes to make sure the filling doesn't burn*.

- If you'd like to make an actual pie out of this recipe or with similar ingredients just augment / grind 450g - 500g of oats. For the filling use 4 apples, 2 cups of mixed berries: [Strawberries, Blueberries, Raspberries] - and then use a pie form instead of a muffin tray - (see image below).

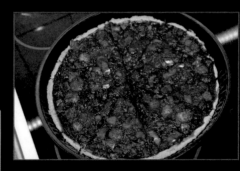

See next page for the nice cream inspiration.

2 Ingredient Nice Cream

Ingredients
2 large frozen ripe Bananas
1/3 tsp of Vanilla powder

Directions

(Preferably frozen unpeeled Bananas, as that creates a creamier consistency). Leave outside of the freezer for a while or leave under running warm water before peeling & blending.
Sprinkle some Vanilla in the mix, and continue blending until you're happy with the result.

This is definitely a lifesaver on a late evening, or movie night.

Keep it very simple sometimes.

Benefits of Vanilla:
Apart from it's ability to reduce startle reflexes, and relieve sleep apnea, it also helps to alleviate respiratory conditions, soothe anxiety, prevent acne, facilitate weight loss, while keeping the growth of cancerous cells & tumors in check, etc.

- For a bit fancier moment, add some berries, cacao nibs, granola, etc.

Sorbet à la eCo

Ingredients

2 large peeled frozen Bananas
1 cup of frozen Mango (yellow)
1 cup of Raspberries (red)
Walnuts
Dried Mango
Raw Agave Syrup
(Buckthorn Berries: optional)

Directions

In a high-speed blender, blend / mix each ingredient separately. (The banana one should have a pinch of vanilla powder in it).

For beautiful shapes, find a form with a spherical shape (I found one of those refrigerator egg-forms that I never use), it worked wonders.

Fill up the form or whatever you have to shape with and freeze for a little while.

When ready, serve on a plate or in a bowl, add a little chocolate sauce & agave / syrup on top (or bottom first), then sprinkle some dried fruit (Mango), nuts (Walnuts), etc. Or why not in a coco wrap with banana split (fried banana)?

That nice looking brown dust all over the sorbet is vanilla powder garnished through a fine strainer mesh with extremely tiny holes (kitchen stainless steel filter), or you can just pinch and sprinkle.

D.I.Y - 3 Ingredient "Chocolate Sauce":

In a small pot: whisk 6 Tbsp of raw cacao, 1/2 a tsp of vanilla, 5 Tbsp of agave / syrup & 1/2 a cup of oat milk on low heat until it becomes a thick chocolate cream (about 3 - 4 minutes, keep stirring / whisking until it thickens). - *Adjust accordingly*.

Why Oat Milk? - It has a natural creamy consistency when heated. No other plant based milk can thicken on its own as oat milk. I've tried quite a few.

Ingredients

80g of Flaxseeds
40g of Chia Seeds
(1/2 a tsp of vegan butter)
50g of Sesame Seeds
A pinch of pink Himalayan Salt
1 tsp of Agave / Syrup (optional)
30g of chopped Pumpkin Seeds

Directions

Preheat oven on maximum level.
Put all the ingredients in a bowl (add hot water a little at a time while stirring with a spoon until the mix looks / feels pretty firm).
Put parchment paper on a tray. Using a spoon, scoop a bit of the mix at a time, put it on the tray and slightly flatten it evenly, into a preferred shape.
Once the bowl is empty, put the tray in the oven on medium heat, and let the crackers heat up / dehydrate for about 25 - 30 minutes,
or until a bit firm enough. (Keep an open eye on the temperature every every now and then). - *They're perfectly crunchy once cooled*.

Seed Crackers

Flaxseeds & Chia Seeds have a natural gel that acts as binding material when soaked.
– How flat should they be? You decide: (See images for inspiration).
– Enjoy it as is, or with soup, guacamole, or why not with one of the dressings in this book. Yum!!
- [These are very crunchy, but if you'd like a bit chewy bread-like consistency, then add 30g of almonds made into flour to the mix].

Be creative with the shapes, feel free, and be playful with this recipe.

Protein & Energy Bombs

Ingredients

100g of Oats
50g of mixed seeds: (sesame, pumpkin, chia)
1/2 a tsp of Extra Virgin Coconut Oil
1 Tbsp of Agave syrup
15 to 18 fresh soft pitted dates
- Optional: [cacao/cinnamon/peanut butter/vanilla]

- (No food processor? No problem, a blender can help or even just hands, but takes some work).

This is a perfect quick snack that not only satisfies the sweet tooth, but it also refills the body with essential nutrients simultaneously!

Directions

Get some Granola, or make your own using 100g of oats and 50g of sesame, pumpkin & chia seeds (or whatever else you like). Put that in a pan on low heat with 1/2 a tsp of coconut oil & agave / syrup (for the crunch) then stir for a few minutes or until a brown / golden color appears.

Put the granola in a food processor together with 15 - 18 fresh soft pitted dates, and turn / pulse carefully until you get a firm mass, (or by hand).

From here you can now make different shapes with their own individual flavors [optional]. Just grab a chunk at a time by hand and add either cinnamon / cacao / peanut butter / vanilla / etc, then mold and put aside.

— Simple as that.

- [If you don't want to heat the granola up, it is not required, you can still achieve good results with raw oats].

There are no limits as to what you can add to this recipe, the most important part is enough binding material (fresh dates), to hold it together.

Oat Crackers – (Nutty & Crunchy)

Ingredients

1 cup of ground oats
1 Tbsp of each seed:
flax, chia & sesame
1 tsp of vegan butter
1 tsp of Agave / syrup
3 - 5 chopped almonds
Some hot water for soaking
1 & 1/2 Tbsp of baking powder
A pinch of pink Himalayan Salt

Directions

Preheat oven.
Putt all the ingredients in a bowl (except for the oat flour & chopped almonds).
Add hot water, little by little while stirring. Then add the oat flour, and keep stirring to
a point where it becomes dough-like, and can be picked up without falling apart or
stick to the fingers.
Now add the chopped almonds and kneed with your hand/s.
You're now ready to cut little pieces and flatten them to your liking, then put them on
a tray with parchment paper on it. Place the tray in the center of the oven, and bake
on medium heat for just 20 - 25 minutes (since the oven has been preheated and is
hot enough). – Allow the crackers to cool completely before enjoying!

The most important part in this recipe, is the firmness of the dough. As long as it is not sticky, you're good to go.
- [If you want to add a little baking powder to make it a bit airy as a regular cookie, you can do it].
The level of salt / sweetness is also up to you.

Choco Sauce D.I.Y on page: 89

Mini Farm: D.I.Y – (Pallet Collar / Raised Bed)

I once decided I wasn't going to mess around ever again, until I've learned how to grow simple crops, to fully heal and write with my left hand again, and also learn to meditate the proper way, etc. It was around 2017. A pretty worthy challenge and every chance I got, I was on it.

I managed to kill a bunch of plants, 2 yrs almost no sign of growth, whatever germinated didn't make it, but my left hand writing kept getting better that it wrote a poetry book, and also my meditations improved as well.

Then eventually I realized a truth that probably takes decades to comprehend.

See that mini wooden pallet collar..? I saw it where I was working and thought I'd just make it even smaller for an experiment that could fit on my porch which started as a joke, but little did I know I was about to become a mini farmer in a small space. If I say that I knew what I was doing, I'd be not telling the truth. Yet it felt like I was being guided to get out of the box through learning something that seemed almost impossible.

Anyhow my semi self-quarantine period sort of paid off - it made me a mini farmer, a photographer, writer of music and poetry - (now with my own meditation poetry book called: **"Spiritual Surgery"**).

My English improved, I became self-made ambidextrous after fully healing my left hand, took meditation to a whole different level (learned the mechanism behind brain waves & energy healing), etc.

Never underestimate the simple things in life, they're the only aspect with the capacity to withstand the test of time.

<< Acquire skills every day, that school or any other institution won't or will never be able to offer, skills no external influence can waver. Your inner guidance will lead you. – It is your birthright! >>

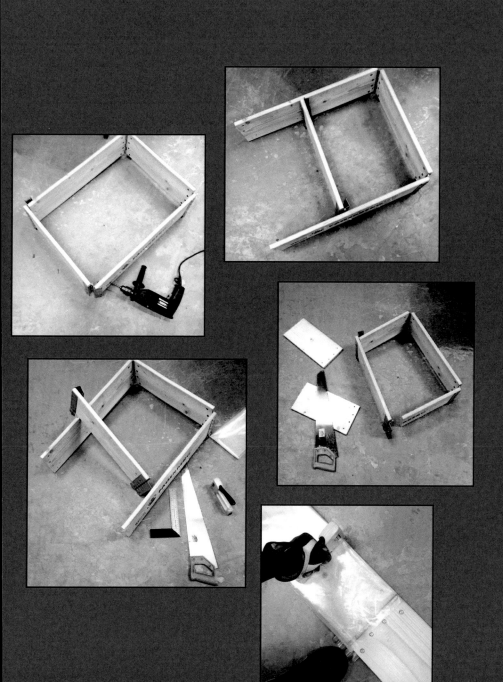

Allow me to brag a little ...

I usually don't brag, but I'll take advantage of this moment to share with you something special about me that I've discovered the past few years of experimenting with and learning from nature.
I'll begin by saying that I'm happy and truly proud of myself, because of the fact that some of the greens in my simple but delicious and healthy recipes are homegrown by yours truly, and also 100% organic.

The skills I've acquired on my front porch will definitely come in handy once I decide to do it on a grander scale.

– As the ancient saying goes: "How you do anything is how you do everything".

I once caught myself complaining about the quality and environmental impact, etc. while doing the groceries every other day. Then asked myself, "what if I could grow at least a few herbs, or why not some leafy greens?" ..I've learned so much just from a little bit of soil and buckets right outside my window than I learned anywhere else the past two decades of my life, though I live in the northern hemisphere, (Sweden).

"While wondering where I'd get the money to build sliding glass doors". After a while I received a letter from the landlord offering to build one, as though they heard my thoughts & wishes. The rent would then be a bit higher but it didn't matter because it felt destined, it felt like an instant manifestation and I was too excited to be worried, more than I had been prior to that moment.

I used to live across the street, was new in town without a job, lots of stress, and one day while looking through the window I wished I lived on the other side (here) since the sun would be more available throughout the day. I really wanted to be able to plant some stuff. Unfortunately I had to relocate (short term contract) to a different area but within a few months I was offered a new contract in the exact same building right across the street from the window I once looked through with a simple wish. It's where I'm writing this book from as we speak & where I learned all of this and more.

Anyhow - I went on.. Many plants died, I almost gave up but then realized that plants are living beings who need the same care as anyone else both physically, and energetically. They're literally alive, after all- without them we wouldn't be able to live on this planet.

Sipping on fresh orange juice while watching little tomatoes growing, thinking "did I really plant food here?" What else can I do? What do we really know as a collective about life & true value on a Planet so rich in soil, air, water, vegetation & more..?

This moment back in 2017 felt almost like an actual dream. I took this picture and forgot about it, then found it some other time and it felt unreal. One moment there's no sign of growth, and a while later tomatoes in my hand. – Magical!

I can confidently confirm that though they look amazing, their juicy appearance doesn't get any where near the taste and quality in comparison.
— Every child should be taught this at least once, while in school. For as humans on this planet; most of the future depends on it.

Looking at my first tomatoes after taking a bite that completely changed my world-view. After tasting these tomatoes & later on my homegrown cucumbers, I was not able to eat store bought veggies for a long time. I felt cheated & deceived!

After a while I felt confident enough to grow cucumbers from scratch. I learned how to pollinate manually using a cotton swab since bees are pretty scarce nowadays, and it worked very well.

The best part is that you get new seeds forever, - literally. Isn't it what life is about? Abundance & infinite prosperity gifted to us by Mother Nature, Universe or God, – you name it. Either way, it's our birthright.

Cherish Seeds ...

Did you know that the average person has no clue that seeds in fruits, and veggies are what actually create the fruits & veggies in the first place? Seeds are thrown in the trash on a daily basis by many people. Either save them, or throw them in the woods, and let the ground do its job.

A 4m² space would suffice for 1 household either using buckets, raised beds, or directly into the ground. Now imagine seeds from a few peppers, they could undoubtedly supply multiple homes with enough veggies to enjoy decent & healthy meals. True freedom is usually found in places that we often fail to look.

[It all starts with a simple seed]: A skill so simple that anyone can master it regardless of age or background, which could reverse the current condition of our planet within a decade or so, if incorporated in schools & communities, etc...

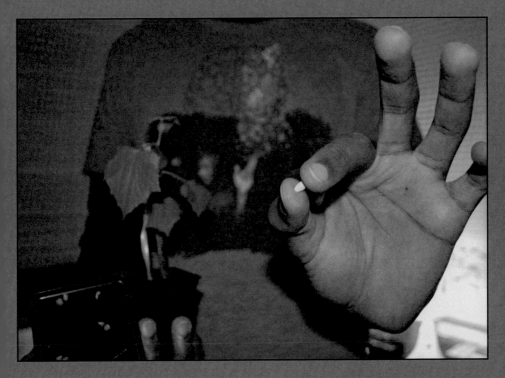

..And from that seed, many others are born indefinitely.
We literally live on a magical planet... and that makes us..?

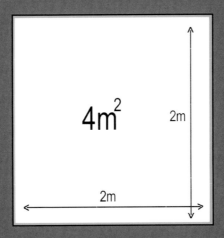

"2020 Vision" turned out literal for me ...

Between the age of 20 & 25, I found myself in front of a screen both at school & home, eyesight deteriorating - (many of my relatives wear glasses).

I immediately made a decision that I'll absolutely not be wearing glasses by the age of 30. I started by getting rid of the TV, alcohol & sugar as a powerful symbol (the worst legal drugs in society), then gave myself 7 to 10 years.
This lead me down a path where nothing was ever the same again, I gained so much wisdom and knowledge about this world especially in regards to health and accidentally became a 'health-guru' in my vicinity.
A decade is a long time, but sometimes it feels like I have the ability to freeze time and jump.

As we already know, the world's health is already worsening with all the Genetically Modified Foods, chemicals, and toxins everywhere.

<< Talking about vision & sight.. according to a study, by 2030 especially in the US, the population will be nearsighted. In other words, people's eyesight will have worsened to the point where wearing eyeglasses will be the new normal for the majority. >>

With a little determination, a lot can be reversed.
The human body is designed to self-correct, and when we get out of its way, magical things begin to happen. The key lies in daring to walk a completely new path in terms of nutrition. We become what we consume after all.

I just didn't see myself with goggles in the future ...

I love my freedom to the point where I don't even wear a wristwatch - heck if I could, I'd walk barefoot all the time. So the thought of having to wear glasses gave me a sense of discomfort. But now I'm free from them among other things I've been able to break free from along the journey.

In Nature

Never underestimate the power of strolling in Nature. It is a perfect opportunity to move the body while breathing cleaner air since trees filter it and have it in abundance. If you can remove your shoes it's even better since the ground has negative ions that our bodies need, and they are absorbed through our feet when in direct contact with soil.
They reduce stress, improve mood, facilitate sleep & increase concentration.

(Psst.. Even touching or hugging a tree provides us with the same benefits).
We could all use some of that goodness especially in these times, for sure.
– Let's get connected!

Why so serious?

As I may have mentioned it before, I'm one of the people who find it hard when it comes to dry fasting for a long time, I can't lie. Instead, I do it intermittently or just find the most medicinal/alkaline fruits/veggies, then eat that as detox, and also make juices. This is actually satisfying rather than stressful, it also allows the body to absorb vitamins and minerals while healing simultaneously.

The body can easily digest fruit since it has its own purified water (see page: 1 - 15), and within a few hours it has been broken down, in comparison to other foods that tend to stay in the gut longer causing various issues down the road; mostly because of dryness and lack of enough fiber/enzymes.

n terms of exercise, there's really no 'one fits all' formula, but what I have realized is that as long as a person moves their body regularly and gets enough oxygen, provided of course they consume similar foods like those found in this book, they can get very far stress free. I'm not a fitness type of guy myself, but a few push-ups and stretching do my body good. I ride a bicycle, walk a lot, do some yoga & meditate because I strongly believe that the mind is the blueprint or the engine; basically where it all begins.

'Be gentle with yourself, and remember to treat yourself as you'd want to be treated by someone who cares about you." – eCo

The Power Under Your Feet

We were programmed to believe that our feet are merely objects to stand on and walk from A to B in this system of coming & going for the sole purpose of movement it seems - until we die, but there's a lot more to these among the most underrated magnificent parts of the body.

Did you know that there are a myriad of nerves in the feet connected to every organ inside of the body as if the feet were some form of remote control? - [The same goes for palms/fingers].

This is why walking barefoot on uneven ground or surface brings homeostasis or balance back into the body. It's like a quick massage, plus negative ions being absorbed simultaneously through the skin and up throughout the entire body.

So next time you walk - mean it, and do so proudly.

Unfortunately based on the way today's footwear/ground are designed, most people's feet do not get an equal amount of pressure on each nerve that is connected to other organs, and this results in a lot of issues later in life.

The best thing would be to avoid shoes that torture feet or that separate them too much from the ground and their natural shape, as this gradually damages the inside in subtle yet impactful ways, mentally/emotionally/physically.. Paving for future traumas.

<< It is scary when you realize that the average person wears some form of shoes up to 20 out of 24 hours. >>

Massaging feet even for a few minutes is probably the healthiest, most convenient and best gift one can receive from oneself or from a significant one, if you are lucky. :)

I prefer adding essential oils, among them: Lemongrass & Lavender. These smell heavenly, they have a powerful healing effect, they calm the nerves while also preventing fungus and other unwanted bugs from thriving.

Essential Oils

I was asked what I think about essential oils.
I've been using them for a while. I've realized most people use them solely for the sake of smelling great which is alright, but there's a lot more to essential oils especially in terms of health benefits, they're very powerful.

My favorite is Lemongrass, I grew up around a lot of such, my mother smelled like fresh ginger & lemongrass.
They can be used when washing clothes or cleaning. Essential oils have been used for thousands of years as medicine and are an absolute perfect substitute for commercial perfume/fragrance/deodorant/.. Synthetic fragrances are packed with poisonous chemicals that shouldn't be anywhere near our noses or skin.
Essential oils smell truly amazing and heal the body/mind at the same time.
- I once entered a room and people went: "Who smells like ginger and lemon? It smells like nature in here!"
- And I was like: "Um.. Hellooo..."

People tend become calmer when they approach me due to the relaxing effect of essential oils, and many of them notice it.

(Do a little research and learn some more about essential oils).
There are many different kinds such as Lavender which most people like (when mixed with lemongrass is perfect for foot baths, whole body baths & massages), also there's Cinnamon, Peppermint, Eucalyptus, Rosemary, Orange, etc...

ATTN. Not to be applied directly to the skin since it's a concentrated liquid, dilute with some water before use. *Always Choose Organic*.

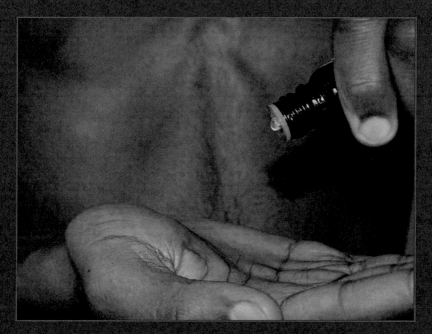

Don't hesitate to try different ones, or even mix a few together, it is very healing. They've been used throughout all ancient civilizations as cosmetics, and also as natural medicine.

Here are some health benefits of Lemongrass Plant:
The leaves and the oil are used to make medicine. Lemongrass is used for treating **digestive tract spasms, stomach-ache, high blood pressure, convulsions, pain, vomiting, cough, achy joints (rheumatism), fever, the common cold, exhaustion, etc**.

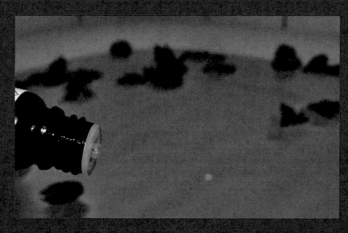

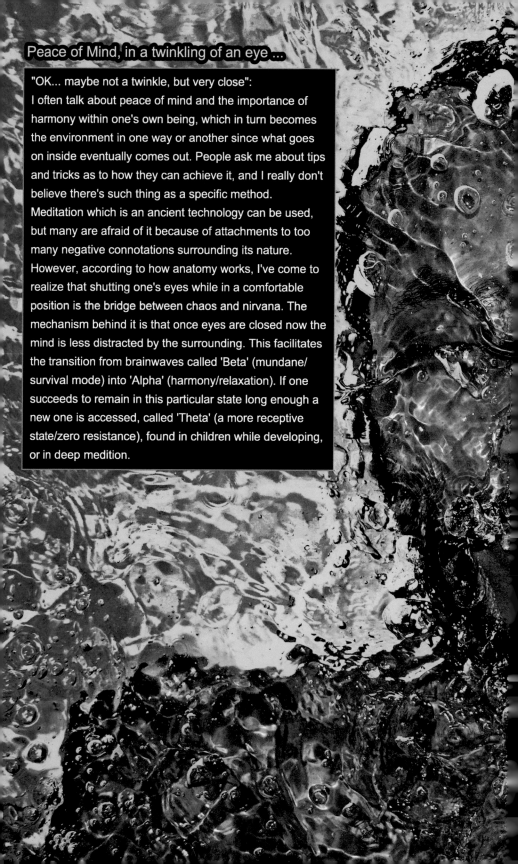

Peace of Mind, in a twinkling of an eye ...

"OK... maybe not a twinkle, but very close":
I often talk about peace of mind and the importance of
harmony within one's own being, which in turn becomes
the environment in one way or another since what goes
on inside eventually comes out. People ask me about tips
and tricks as to how they can achieve it, and I really don't
believe there's such thing as a specific method.
Meditation which is an ancient technology can be used,
but many are afraid of it because of attachments to too
many negative connotations surrounding its nature.
However, according to how anatomy works, I've come to
realize that shutting one's eyes while in a comfortable
position is the bridge between chaos and nirvana. The
mechanism behind it is that once eyes are closed now the
mind is less distracted by the surrounding. This facilitates
the transition from brainwaves called 'Beta' (mundane/
survival mode) into 'Alpha' (harmony/relaxation). If one
succeeds to remain in this particular state long enough a
new one is accessed, called 'Theta' (a more receptive
state/zero resistance), found in children while developing,
or in deep medition.

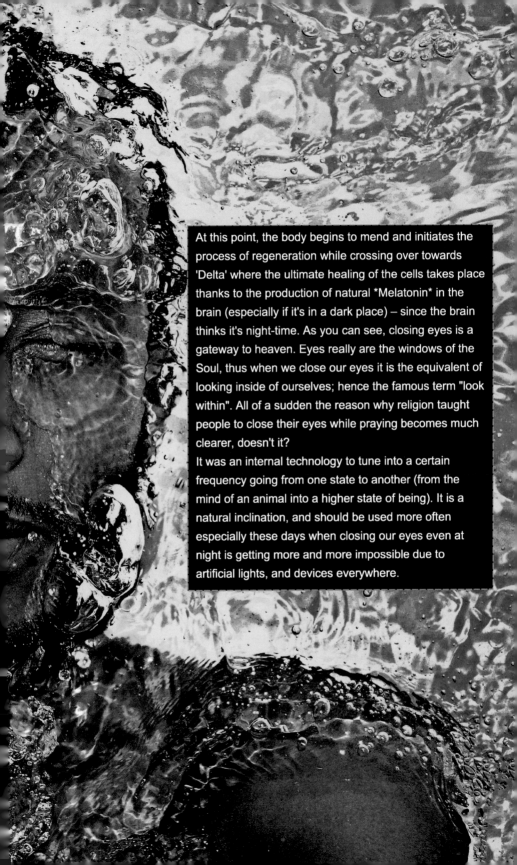

At this point, the body begins to mend and initiates the process of regeneration while crossing over towards 'Delta' where the ultimate healing of the cells takes place thanks to the production of natural *Melatonin* in the brain (especially if it's in a dark place) – since the brain thinks it's night-time. As you can see, closing eyes is a gateway to heaven. Eyes really are the windows of the Soul, thus when we close our eyes it is the equivalent of looking inside of ourselves; hence the famous term "look within". All of a sudden the reason why religion taught people to close their eyes while praying becomes much clearer, doesn't it?

It was an internal technology to tune into a certain frequency going from one state to another (from the mind of an animal into a higher state of being). It is a natural inclination, and should be used more often especially these days when closing our eyes even at night is getting more and more impossible due to artificial lights, and devices everywhere.

Meditation for Healing & Regeneration

"**What is MEDITATION?**": I get this question a lot, I decided I'd try to make a somewhat simplistic visual version of the process. See, first one must understand the different brain waves that run our lives.

In my own experiences, stage one represents the brain waves 'Beta': 14 - 30 Hz (mundane/survival mode/control). We're here most of the time because it is easier to hide in the noise rather than face what's going on within, which could help us mend & live in constant harmony with nature free from perpetual fears, afflictions & illnesses.

Stage 1:
Once we've acknowledged this societal standard & chaotic state, we are ready to relinquish the attachment to external distractions regardless of how rewarding they may be, we then move into 'Alpha': 9 - 13 Hz (relaxation/preparation for higher states). This begins with a simple thing that is becoming more & more impossible today, which is: *closing the eyes*.

Stage 2:
When we've learned to stay here long enough, we unlock 'Theta' brain waves: 4 - 8 Hz, which is a state of surrender (non-resistance/receptive). It is a frequency which children up to 13 years of age naturally operate on (great for hypnosis & programming/reprogramming of the mind). In this state, the healing process kicks in among other things.

Stage 3:
When the resistance has been fully relinquished, the barrier breaks creating a bridge that leads into 'Delta': 0,5 - 4 Hz (regeneration/deep sleep/no longer in the body). At this point *Melatonin* flows freely through, and other bodily corrections take place. Basically, the driver [YOU] is no longer in control.

<< Remember to close your eyes more often, it trains your brain to enter the mind-states mentioned previously much easier like a child when you go to bed. Most people do not reach that state because they go to sleep in a hurry or while still upset due to mental exhaustion. If you're familiar with the teachings of Christ, he said [Matt. 18:3]: "only children can inherit the Kingdom of God". It was more about the mind [Theta/Delta state] than a place beyond the sky. God is in all of us, hence [Luke 17:21]: "Heaven is within YOU"; so claim it today. – The body really is a temple of God, take great care of it. >>

118

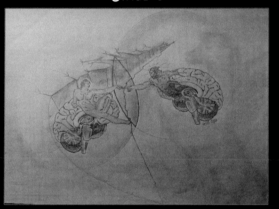

I decided to depict 'Beta' as Yang/Masculine since the characteristics are similar to those of the left brain (rigid) & the higher states as Yin/Feminine, right brain (nurturing creative force).

At stage 3 the left & right hemispheres meet within the Vesica Piscis that resembles a womb (rebirth/regeneration,- hence the water) & it also looks like an eye (3rd eye/Pineal Gland where *Melatonin* is produced). This is the Biblical garden or land that flows with milk & honey. – Art, excerpt from: *"Spiritual Surgery"* - by Eddy Coleson.

F.Y.I - Research *"Brain Waves"* – learn how they affect our perception, our choices, how they even determine how we live our daily lives & future as a collective.

Like most people who love animals especially very small ones such as butterflies, bees, ladybugs, etc. I've always wanted to be able to interact or at least touch one without accidentally causing harm since these are very sensitive animals not only physically but also energetically. Anyhow, I've never been able to make any insect feel safe enough to approach me let alone land on my hand, plus all the negative beliefs in the subconscious about insects that of course work as limitations creating the gap between me & the animals.

It's not until I started meditating regularly, and doing some gardening around the house that I realized something absolutely mind blowing. Whenever I'd be relaxed with very little to no active thought passing through my mind especially in terms of worries – then birds, bees, butterflies, cats, etc. would show up on my porch. It looked random until on beautiful sunny day I said to myself: "this butterfly seems to keep returning, it's probably not the same one but it'd really be amazing if I could get close enough so that I can take a picture".

The next day it came back and I couldn't believe my eyes when I approached it and it did not move, I ran inside to get my camera and a while later I just spontaneously said: "do you mind climbing on my finger beautiful butterfly..?"

I don't know if it heard or understood what I was saying but it literally flew across the area, and came straight to my left hand. It allowed me to take pictures and when I said: "thank you little butterfly, go ahead and fly away if you want to."

After this experience, the more calmness I achieved inside of me, newer animals kept appearing as if to say: "you're doing great eCo, keep it up!"

This really was a powerful sign of restoration, I am more than grateful because I've been able to share with others which has brought joy and also put a smile on many faces; and hopefully yours too.

‑ BTW, did you know that without insects especially BEES, humanity would not exist? They're responsible for pollination which is how more plants are born all around us in our environment. So thank the bees whenever you see them, they're literally our heroes.

I personally realized the importance of bees when my cucumbers kept withering away, apparently they needed bees to move pollen from the male cucumbers to the female ones or simply from other plants. So I learned how to do it manually whenever bees were scarce. It works like a charm, however insects do it more efficiently and way faster than a human can, it's their main assignment and purpose after all.

Energy Management

We've all once, or perhaps even twice been in that place of complete despair. Lack of motivation, energy depletion, paralysis, etc. This can be traced back to its roots which is always *fear* that's been brewing gradually waiting for the perfect moment to strike. Strangely enough in the word "FEAR", hidden in it is found another word that spells "REAF". And according to the dictionary, the meaning of reaf is "robber" or "thief".

– So whenever someone or something instills or stimulates fear in you, it is stealing from you. What is being stolen? *Life Force*, Energy! And this happens in tiny quantities until one is depleted, (because of how the body functions.. If it is not repairing cells, it is in fight or flight mode = Energy Extraction).

In the fight or flight state, the body is operating in what is Medically known as the "Sympathetic Nervous System", (survival mode). What we want is the "Parasympathetic Nervous System", which is the exact opposite, it is a relaxed state. Doesn't this sound like the differences in brain waves mentioned earlier (page: 116 - 119) where I explain what Meditation does?

Allow nothing or no one to send you into these states of mind that take from you rather add to your well being.

<< Very few simple movements synchronized with your breath, coming from the diaphragm through the nose can activate a version of you that has the potential to overcome circumstances that'd otherwise seem impossible; without attachments to negative emotions. >>
- There's a magical power in relaxation, it literally changes a person's perception & way of thinking.

Pause the thinking & just move with the flow, even for 3 minutes ...
[Whether you dance, jump, stretch, etc.] - Just Do It!

When a person is underwater, all of a sudden they're fully aware of everything, they pay 100% attention to their breath, a slight mistake could end their life in a matter of seconds. This level of awareness should also be applied on land to a certain extent, there should be a certain way of moving in alignment & harmony with the breath, like other species do naturally.

Breathing wrong paves for the activation of the Sympathetic Nervous System, which sends a signal to the brain saying that a person is being chased or is at war, forcing the body to create stress hormones throwing the entire system off.

So moving the body while breathing deep has a tremendously powerful effect on our overall health. Especially since most people shallow breathe, which deprives the brain of oxygen, and slows down our healing & regeneration.

Summary

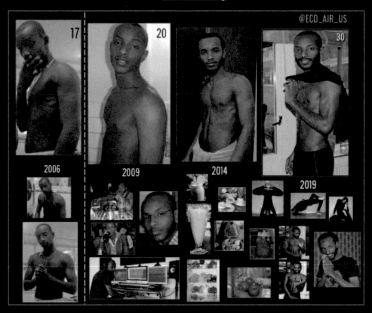

Though without any major health issues, it was probably the most unexpected vision & dream at the age of 15 up to 17. After witnessing almost everyone I knew transform and deteriorate, I realized there might have been something I was missing and unless I did something about it - I was going to be next.

I paid attention to what others were doing especially the adults around me, the things that they had in common, and I chose to do the opposite or completely avoided it.

It was not easy letting go of foods, drinks, and other aspects that are perceived as the norm in society, but I knew it was the right path for me because today almost a decade later, those who looked at me strange back then are the same people who turn to me for information and inspiration.

– Before fitting into society I grew up mostly on fruits & nuts in the heart of Africa, nobody understood it except for my mother who also was mostly vegetarian unknowingly - (she was not fond of meats & couldn't bare the smell of fish, especially while cooking). That being said, I'm excited and truly proud of myself for resurrecting the child within, my body knew what it needed from the get go. Never underestimate your inner voice, it knows way more than you can imagine; better listen!

It's TRUE! You Are What You Eat:

1993 / 94

1997 / 98

2022

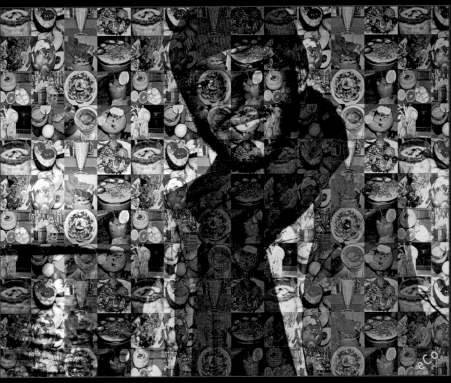

I made this image about half a decade ago when I heard or read somewhere that: "we become what we consume, especially in the form of nutrition". I'm glad to have come across this saying, because I couldn't have said it any better myself. Life is really amazing and has so much for us to discover when we decide to take the first step no matter where we are or even how uncertain we may be at the moment.

I conclude this journey with you by saying thank you very much for deciding to choose my book. I couldn't thank you enough and I hope it brings value into your daily life so that you can also share with others all the amazing things contained in it.

Hopefully one beautiful day I'll get to hear your feedback directly, which would be worth more than gold. Until then, continue taking great care of your wonderful temple (body), it's your most valuable asset in this physical reality, it can't be replaced, but everything else can.

– Wishing you the best & stay well.

Credit & Other Sources

(100% Vegan, Gluten-Free & Organic Coconut Wraps):
- Company: Nuco
- Facebook: NUCO - Coconuts For Life
- Instagram: @cocobynuco

Groceries:
- Company: Coop Sverige
- Instagram: @coopsverige
- Facebook: @coop

Inspiration:
(Choosing Organic & Raw-Food) - "Kristina Carrillo-Bucaram":
- Instagram: @fullyrawkristina
- Facebook: @FullyRaw

Plain Celery Juice:
"Anthony William" (Medical Medium)
- Facebook: @Medical Medium
- Instagram: @medicalmedium

Quotes:
- "You Are What You Eat": Anthelme Brillat-Savarin, 1826 – [The Physiology of Taste].

- "How You Do Anything, Is How You Do Everything". – Zen Buddhist

- "Be gentle with yourself, and remember to treat yourself as you'd want to be treated by someone who cares about you." – eCo

Contact

- Author: Eddy Coleson
- E-Mail: eddy.coleson@gmail.com
- Facebook: Eddy Coleson (eCo)
- Instagram: @eCo_Air_Us

Index

Notes

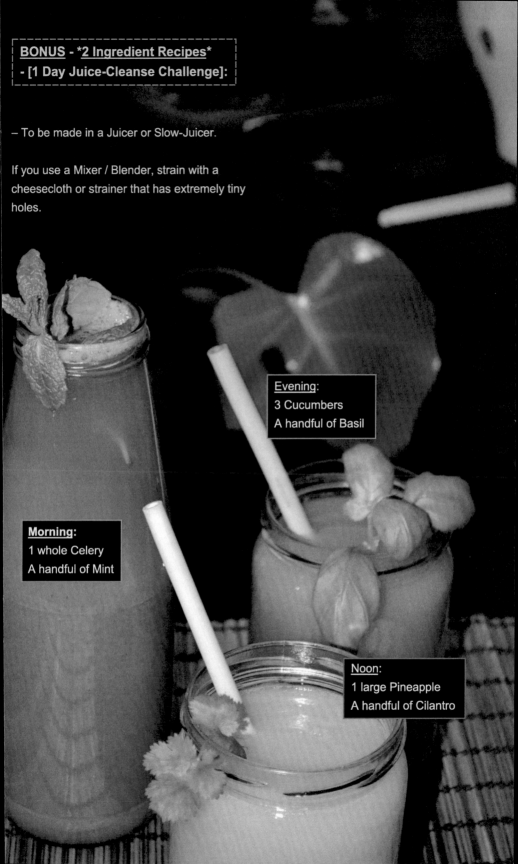

BONUS - *2 Ingredient Recipes*
- [1 Day Juice-Cleanse Challenge]:

– To be made in a Juicer or Slow-Juicer.

If you use a Mixer / Blender, strain with a
cheesecloth or strainer that has extremely tiny
holes.

Evening:
3 Cucumbers
A handful of Basil

Morning:
1 whole Celery
A handful of Mint

Noon:
1 large Pineapple
A handful of Cilantro

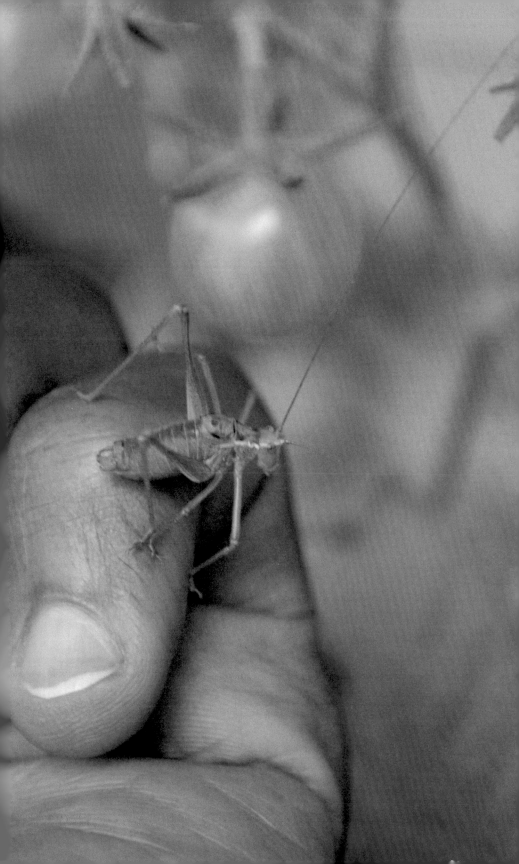

Milton Keynes UK
Ingram Content Group UK Ltd.
UKRC031849280424
441852UK00010B/42